Stellar Science Projects
About
Earth's Sky

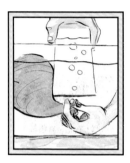

ROBERT GARDNER

ILLUSTRATIONS BY TOM LABAFF

Enslow Elementary
an imprint of

Enslow Publishers, Inc.
40 Industrial Road
Box 398
Berkeley Heights, NJ 07922
USA

http://www.enslow.com

Enslow Elementary, an imprint of Enslow Publishers, Inc.

Enslow Elementary® is a registered trademark of Enslow Publishers, Inc.

Library of Congress Cataloging-in-Publication Data

Gardner, Robert, 1929–
    Stellar science projects about Earth's sky / Robert Gardner.
       p. cm. — (Rockin' Earth science experiments)
    Includes bibliographical references and index.
    ISBN-13: 978-0-7660-2732-9
    ISBN-10: 0-7660-2732-5
    1. Sky—Experiments—Juvenile literature. 2. Science projects—Juvenile literature. I. Title.
  II. Series: Gardner, Robert, 1929–   Rockin' Earth science experiments.
    QC863.5.G37 2007
    551.5078—dc22

                        2006013790

Printed in the United States of America

10 9 8 7 6 5 4 3 2

To Our Readers: We have done our best to make sure all Internet Addresses in this book were active and appropriate when we went to press. However, the author and the publisher have no control over and assume no liability for the material available on those Internet sites or on other Web sites they may link to. Any comments or suggestions can be sent by e-mail to comments@enslow.com or to the address on the back cover.

Illustration credits: Tom LaBaff

Photo credits: Above the Clouds, Inc., p. 45; Enslow Publishers, p. 12; Historic NWS Collection/ NOAA, p. 32; © 2006 Jupiter Images Corporation, pp. 8, 24, 28; NASA Jet Propulsion Laboratory (NASA-JPL), p. 20; NASA and ESA and The Hubble Heritage Team (STScl/AURA), p. 40; P. Parviainen/Photo Researchers, Inc., p. 36; Shutterstock, p. 17.

Cover photo: Shutterstock

Contents

Experiments with a 🎖 symbol feature **Ideas for Your Science Fair.**

Introduction

Go outside and look up! You will see the sky. If it is daytime, you may see a blue sky, the sun, and some puffy, white clouds. (**Never look at the sun! It can hurt your eyes!**) If the sun is setting, the sky may be a brilliant red. Or you may see a sky filled with dark clouds. Raindrops or snowflakes may be falling from the sky.

At night, you may see stars set against a dark sky. The moon that appears to change shape from night to night may also be there. As the seasons change, so do the stars. Different stars appear in the sky. But what is the sky? Why does it change so much? By doing the experiments in this book, you will learn a lot about Earth's sky.

Entering a Science Fair

Most of the experiments in this book (those marked with a 🎗 symbol) have ideas for science fair projects. However, judges at science fairs like experiments that are creative, so do not simply copy an experiment from this book. Take one of the ideas suggested and develop a project of your own. Choose something you really like and want to know more about. It will be more interesting to you. And it can lead to a creative experiment that you plan and carry out.

Before entering a science fair, read one or more of the books about this subject listed under Further Reading. They will give you helpful hints and lots of useful information about science fairs.

Safety First

To do experiments safely always follow these rules:

1 Always do experiments under adult supervision.
2 Read all instructions carefully. If you have questions, check with the adult.
3 Be serious when experimenting. Fooling around can be dangerous to you and to others.
4 Keep the area where you work clean and organized. When you have finished, clean up and put all of your materials away.

Our Sky and Air

On a clear day, the sky looks like a big blue dome. We live under the sky in a sea of air. What do you think air is? Do you think it takes up space? Write down your ideas and your reasons for them.

Now Let's Find Out!

1 Put a wad of cotton on the bottom of a small drinking glass. Turn the glass upside down. The cotton should not fall out.

2 Push the upside-down glass to the bottom of a dishpan filled with water. Does water go into the glass?

3 Lift the glass from the water with one hand. Keep your other hand dry. Touch the cotton with a dry finger. Is the cotton still dry? What does this tell you about air?

THINGS YOU WILL NEED:

- cotton
- small drinking glass
- dishpan
- water
- an adult or friend
- balloon

4 Turn the glass upside down. Push it down into the dishpan. Then turn it sideways under the water. What happens? Was it really empty?

cotton

water

5 Fill the glass with water. Have someone hold the open end of the water-filled glass under water.

6 Blow up a balloon. Hold the neck of the balloon under the mouth of the glass. Slowly let air out of the balloon. What happens?

Our Sky and Air
An Explanation

The cotton stayed dry because the glass was filled with air. Air is a gas. It takes up space.

When the glass was turned sideways, bubbles of air came out. The glass was not empty! It had air in it. A glass full of air weighs less than a glass full of water. The lighter air rose up through the heavier water.

Air in the balloon bubbled up to the top of the glass. Air, like a block of wood, floats on water. The air collected at

FACT: Wind is moving air. It can push on things and move them.

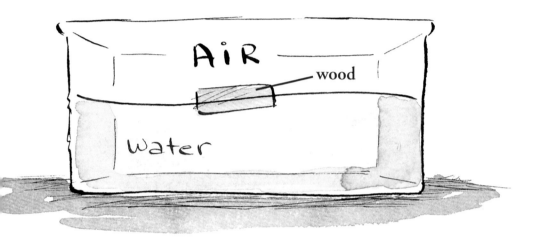

Air and wood both float on water.

the top of the glass. It took up space. It pushed water out the bottom.

The sky is really air, many miles thick. Beyond the air is empty space that reaches to the moon, sun, and stars.

Does Air Have Weight?

Does air have weight? Write down your ideas and your reasons for them.

THINGS YOU WILL NEED:

- **an adult**
- needle valve used to inflate balls
- basketball
- scale or balance that can weigh to the nearest gram or tenth of an ounce
- pencil and paper
- air pump
- 2 yardsticks or 6-ft ruler

Now Let's Find Out!

Have an adult help you with this experiment.

1 Put a needle valve in a basketball. Put your ear near the valve. You should hear air leaving the ball.

2 Wait until you can hear no more air leaving the ball. Then remove the valve and weigh the ball on a scale. The scale should be able to weigh things to the nearest gram or tenth of an ounce. Write the total weight on a piece of paper.

3 Using the valve and a pump, put air into the ball. Inflate the ball until it is very hard.

4 Remove the valve from the ball. The inflated ball should bounce well. (A regulation basketball should bounce to a height of at least 40 inches [102 centimeters] when dropped from a height of 72 inches [183 centimeters].)

5 Now that a lot of air has been added to the ball, weigh the ball again. Write its new weight on the paper. Has the ball's weight changed? What does this tell you about air?

Does Air Have Weight?

An Explanation

The basketball probably weighed 1 or 2 ounces (30–60 grams) more after you pumped more air into it. Adding air made the ball heavier, so air must have weight. In fact, one liter of ordinary air at sea level weighs about 1.29 grams ($\frac{1}{20}$ oz).

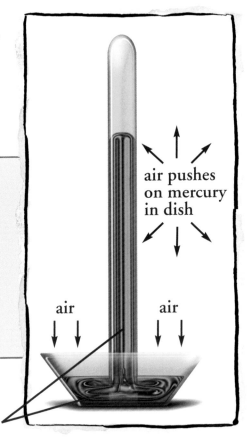

air pushes on mercury in dish

air

air

mercury

FACT: This is a mercury barometer. At sea level, the weight of the air can push a column of mercury (a very heavy liquid) to a height of 30 inches (76 centimeters).

Idea for Your Science Fair 🎗

- Weigh an air-filled balloon on a balance. Break the balloon with a pin. Does the weight of the balloon change?

- Do an experiment to show that air weighed in air seems to have no weight. Is the same true of water weighed in water?

Does Air Push on Things?

Does air push on things? Write down your ideas and your reasons for them.

Now Let's Find Out!

1 Find a clear, empty, rigid plastic bottle with a narrow neck. Put a balloon inside the bottle. Pull the lip of the balloon over the mouth of the bottle. (See the drawing.)

2 Can you blow up the balloon? Can an adult blow it up?

3 **Ask an adult** to make a small hole in the bottom of the bottle. He or she can use a small drill bit or a nail.

THINGS YOU WILL NEED:
- an adult
- clear, empty, rigid plastic bottle with a narrow neck, such as a softsoap refill bottle
- balloon
- small drill bit and drill, or a nail

4 Again, try to blow up the balloon. Why do you think you can blow it up now?

5 Blow up the balloon again. Put your finger over the hole in the bottle. Then take your mouth away from the balloon. Why does the balloon stay inflated? What happens when you remove your finger from the hole? Why does that happen?

Does Air Push on Things?
An Explanation

Because air has weight and takes up space, it pushes on things.

At first, you couldn't blow up the balloon. When you tried, the air in the bottle was squeezed together. It pushed back against the balloon.

Air in the closed bottle pushes against the balloon.

With a hole in the bottle, you inflated the balloon. As the balloon grew, its air pushed the bottle's air out through the hole.

With your finger on the hole, the balloon

If air can be pushed throu a hole, you c blow up the balloon. The balloon can push air out the bottle.

did not empty. But a small amount of air did leave the balloon. The balloon got a little smaller. Then the air in the bottle took up more space. Its push became less than the push of the air in the balloon. So the balloon stayed inflated.

Idea for Your Science Fair

- Have an adult make a hole in the bottom of a plastic bottle, and a second hole near the top of the bottle. Fill the bottle with water. Put the cap back on the bottle. How can you control the flow of water from the bottle? Hint: Put your finger on the hole near the top of the bottle.

FACT: This dirt-carrying truck weighs thousands of pounds. The air in the tires of this huge vehicle pushes outward on the tires. The tires are able to hold up the truck and allow it to roll along smoothly with a full load.

Why Is the Sky Blue?

4

THINGS YOU WILL NEED:

- clear glass jar
- warm water
- dark room
- frosted lightbulb
- a friend
- powdered nondairy creamer
- drinking straw

Why is the sky blue? Write down your ideas and your reasons for them.

Now Let's Find Out!

1 Fill a clear glass jar with warm water. Take it into a dark room where one frosted lightbulb is on.

2 Have a friend hold the jar a foot or two in front of the lightbulb. Look at the lightbulb through the water (see drawing a). Then stand on the other side of the jar from your friend (see drawing b). Again look at the jar.

3 Add a pinch of powdered nondairy creamer to the water. Stir with a straw to thoroughly mix it with the water.

a.

4 Again, stand on the other side of the jar from your friend. Notice that the water has a bluish color when seen from the side. How might this be similar to what makes the sky blue?

frosted bulb

b.

Why Is the Sky Blue?
An Explanation

Sunlight is white, but it has all the colors in a rainbow—violet, blue, green, yellow, orange, and red. When sunlight goes through Earth's blanket of air, particles of air and dust soak up some of the light. They take up a lot of cool colors (mostly blue and some green). They soak up very little of the warm colors (reds and oranges). Then they release the mostly blue light in all directions. We say the blue light is scattered. The scattered light makes the sky look blue.

FACT: The blanket of air on Mars is different from Earth's. As a result, it scatters light differently. That is why the Martian sky you see here is not blue. It is pinkish.

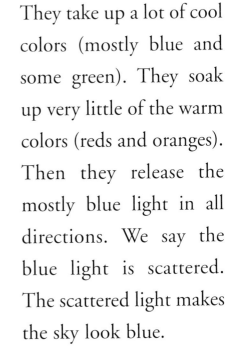

The powder acts like particles of air and dust. When you look at the glass from the side, you see the scattered blue light.

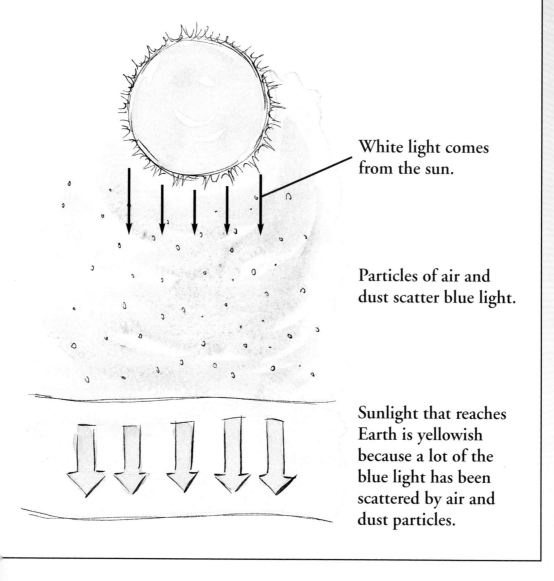

White light comes from the sun.

Particles of air and dust scatter blue light.

Sunlight that reaches Earth is yellowish because a lot of the blue light has been scattered by air and dust particles.

Why Are Sunsets Red?

THINGS YOU WILL NEED:

- clear glass jar
- warm water
- dark room
- frosted lightbulb
- a friend
- powdered nondairy creamer
- drinking straw

Why are sunsets red? Write down your ideas and your reasons for them.

Now Let's Find Out!

1 Fill a clear glass jar with warm water. Take it into a dark room where one frosted lightbulb is on.

2 Hold the jar a foot or two in front of the lightbulb. Look at the lightbulb through the water. What is the color of the light coming from the lightbulb?

3 Add a pinch of powdered nondairy creamer to the water in the jar. Stir with a straw until the powder is thoroughly mixed with the water.

4 Again, look at the lightbulb through the water. What is the color of the light you see coming from the lightbulb? How has the color changed?

5 Add another pinch of nondairy creamer to the water and stir. Look at the lightbulb through the water. What is the color of the light you see coming from the lightbulb? Has the color changed?

6 Continue to add small amounts of the powder. Continue to look at the lightbulb through the water. Does the light you see coming from the bulb ever become red like a setting sun?

Why Are Sunsets Red?
An Explanation

As sunset nears, sunlight's path through the air gets longer (see drawing). By the time the sunlight reaches the ground, most of the cool colors (violet, blue, and green) have been scattered. Only the warmer colors (red, orange, and yellow), especially red, get through the air. As a result, the sun has a reddish color. So do the clouds that reflect the sunlight. The scattering of sunlight by the air makes beautiful sunsets.

The creamer acts like the air and dust. It scatters the cool colors and lets through the warmer colors. Adding more creamer represents a longer path of sunlight through air.

FACT: Beautiful sunsets are caused by the air surrounding Earth. It scatters the cooler colors in sunlight more than the warmer ones.

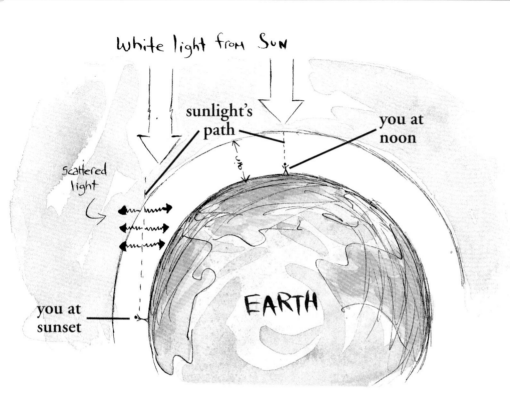

White light from Sun

sunlight's path

you at noon

scattered light

EARTH

you at sunset

Idea for Your Science Fair

- How can a large fish tank, a slide projector, and nondairy creamer be used to show how light is scattered to make a blue sky or a red sunset?

- Is there any truth about weather in the old saying:

Red sky at night, sailors delight;
Red sky in morning, sailors take warning.

6

Make a Cloud

Clouds are often seen in the sky. How are clouds made? Write down your ideas and your reasons for them.

Now Let's Find Out!

1 Find a clear, empty, 2-liter, plastic soda bottle. Pour ½ cup of warm water into the bottle. Screw on the cap. Then shake the bottle.

2 Hold the bottle in front of a well-lighted window. Shake the bottle again. Squeeze the bottle hard. Then suddenly release your squeeze. The pressure inside the bottle will suddenly decrease. Did you see a cloud? Something needed to make a cloud must be missing.

3 Remove the cap from the bottle. **Ask an adult** to light a match, blow it out, and quickly lower the match into the bottle.

THINGS YOU WILL NEED:

- **an adult**
- clear, empty, 2-liter, plastic soda bottle with cap
- measuring cup
- warm water
- well-lighted window
- matches

Now, smoke particles will be inside the bottle. Quickly screw the cap back on.

4 Shake the bottle again. Hold it up against a well-lighted window. Squeeze it hard and then suddenly release your squeeze. Did you see a cloud form this time?

What else was needed to make a cloud?

Make a Cloud
An Explanation

A cloud could form only after smoke was added to your bottle. Why was that so? Smoke particles serve as places where water droplets in the air can collect. Because clouds are made of many tiny water droplets, the smoke in the bottle allowed a cloud to form.

FACT: High cirrus clouds like these are made of tiny ice crystals. They may form ahead of thicker clouds that bring rain or snow.

High above the ground, the push from air (air pressure) is less, so the air expands. Expanding air gets colder. That's what happened when you released the squeeze on your bottle. But cold temperatures are not enough. Water vapor (water as a gas) needs small particles to collect on. The smoke provided the particles.

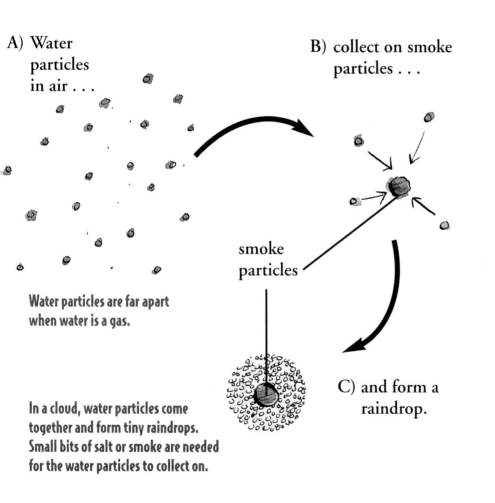

A) Water particles in air . . .

B) collect on smoke particles . . .

smoke particles

C) and form a raindrop.

Water particles are far apart when water is a gas.

In a cloud, water particles come together and form tiny raindrops. Small bits of salt or smoke are needed for the water particles to collect on.

7

Looking for Clouds

Often, you can see clouds in the sky. Do you think some clouds are different from others? Write down your ideas and your reasons for them.

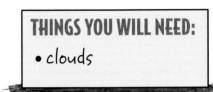

Now Let's Find Out!

Look for clouds. On a perfectly clear day, you will see only blue sky. On other days, you might see fluffy, white clouds. They may look like heaps of loose cotton. These are cumulus clouds. In what kind of weather do you see cumulus clouds?

On some days you might see thin, wispy, feathery clouds. These are cirrus clouds. Some people call these clouds mares' tails. Why? Because they look like the long, thin hair of a horse's tail.

You might find the sky covered with a gray blanket of clouds. These are stratus clouds. When stratus clouds are close to the ground, they are called fog. In what kind of weather do you see stratus clouds?

Looking for Clouds
An Explanation

Cumulus clouds are fair weather clouds. They are usually seen on clear days. On warm, humid days they may grow very tall and become thunderstorms.

Cirrus clouds may also be seen on clear days, but they, too, may thicken and bring rain or snow.

Cumulus clouds

Cirrus clouds

Stratus clouds are usually not very high and often bring rain or snow.

Stratus clouds

Idea for Your Science Fair 🎀

- Cirrus, cumulus, and stratus are the three basic types of clouds, but there are others. Find out what they are and look for them. Take photographs of them. How can they help you predict the weather?

FACT: This giant cloud is called a cumulonimbus cloud or a thunderhead. A thunderstorm is likely to develop within such a cloud.

8

Directions from a Star

Do you think stars can give directions? Write down your ideas and your reasons for them.

Now Let's Find Out!

1 On a clear night, look for the Big Dipper. It is a group of stars that looks like a dipper (see the drawing). An adult may be able to help you. The dipper may be turned differently than in the drawing. Slowly turn the book all the way around. It could be in any of the positions you saw.

2 Merak and Dubhe are pointer stars. Imagine a line connecting Merak to Dubhe. Extend that line five times as far as the distance between Merak and Dubhe. You will be looking at the North Star (Polaris). It is the last star on the handle of the Little Dipper.

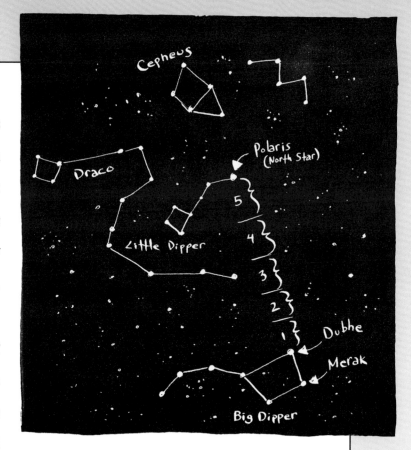

3 The North Star is above Earth's North Pole. The direction north is under the North Star. Now find south, east, and west.

4 Find the other groups of stars in the drawing. These groups are called constellations. On another night, look at these constellations every hour from dark until you go to bed. The constellations seem to move. Can you explain why?

5 Find these constellations at about the same time at least once a week. Do this for several months. How do the constellations seem to move over time? Why?

Constellations near the North Star

Directions from a Star
An Explanation

The North Star shows you where north is. To find other directions, face north. South is behind you. East is on your right; west is on your left.

Constellations near the North Star can be seen all year. They seem to move slowly around the North Star during the night. Why? Because Earth turns around once every 24 hours.

If you look at these stars at the same time every night, their positions change. Why?

FACT: A camera was pointed toward the North Star. Its shutter was left open for hours. The bright lines show the circular paths of the northern stars as seen from Earth.

Because Earth moves slowly around the sun—once each year. As a result, the stars seen at the same time seem to move slowly. The drawing shows the Big Dipper at 9 P.M. on January 15, April 15, July 15, and October 15.

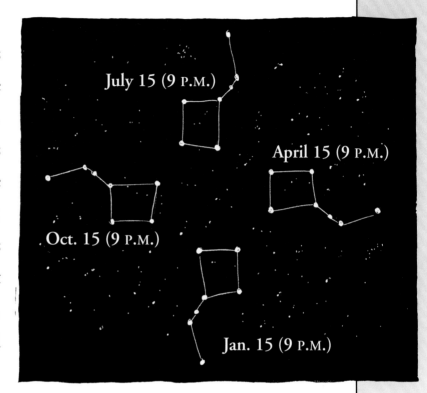

Ideas for Your Science Fair

- How could you use the North Star to find the latitude of your home?

- How could you find directions in the southern hemisphere?

- Make a model to show why constellations near the North Star can be seen all year.

9

Stars Near and Far

Suppose you see two stars in the sky that look equal in brightness. Does that mean they are the same distance from Earth? Write down your ideas and your reasons for them.

Now Let's Find Out!

Do this experiment in a large dark room or basement.

THINGS YOU WILL NEED:

- an adult
- large dark room or basement
- 2 lamps
- table
- 2 frosted lightbulbs, 25 watts and 100 watts

1 **Ask an adult** to put two lamps side by side on a table. Put a 25-watt frosted lightbulb in one lamp. Put a 100-watt frosted lightbulb in the other lamp. The lightbulbs represent stars of different brightness.

2 Stand about 20 feet from the lightbulbs. Which lightbulb appears brighter?

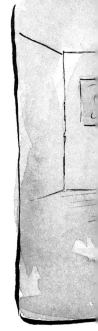

3 **Ask the adult** to slowly move the lamp with the dimmer bulb toward you. Does the dimmer bulb begin to look brighter?

4 Tell the adult to stop when the two bulbs look equally bright. How far is each lightbulb from you now? What does this experiment tell you about star brightness and distance?

Stars Near and Far
An Explanation

You used two lightbulbs. One was brighter than the other. But they appeared equally bright when the dimmer bulb was closer. The same is true of stars. Stars of equal brightness may not be the same distance from Earth.

An airplane passing a bright star will look close to the star. But it is much closer to Earth than the star. The moon, too, can appear close to a star. But it is only about 250,000 miles (more than 400,000 km) from Earth. Stars are trillions of miles from Earth. We simply can't judge the distance to objects in the sky.

FACT: This photo was taken by the Hubble Space Telescope. The telescope can show us distant parts of the sky not visible to our eyes.

The "Ant Nebula" is a dying star.

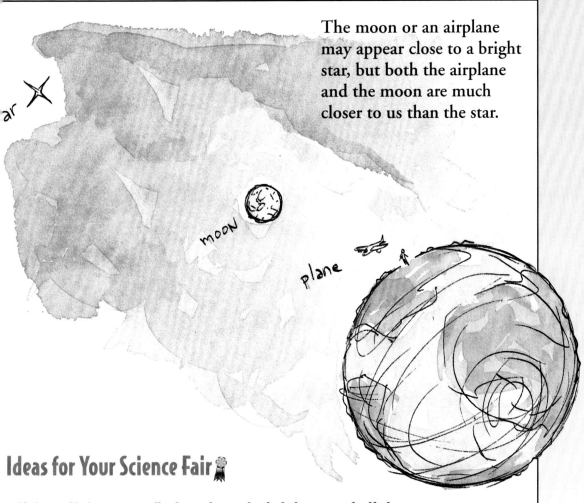

The moon or an airplane may appear close to a bright star, but both the airplane and the moon are much closer to us than the star.

Ideas for Your Science Fair

- Using a light meter, find out how the brightness of a light appears to change if you double the distance from it.

- Astronomers refer to a star's brightness as a magnitude. What is meant by a star's magnitude? What magnitude stars can you see?

10

Balloons, Sky, and Water

A big, colorful, hot air balloon floating in the sky is a beautiful sight. People may be in the basket beneath the balloon. Can you make a hot air balloon? Write down your ideas and your reasons for them.

Now Lets Find Out!

You will need two adults to help you with this experiment.

1 In a large garage or basement, **have an adult** hold the open end of a thin (0.5 mil), large trash bag over an electric hot plate. She should wear gloves and be careful not to let the bag touch the heater. You can hold up the closed end of the bag so that hot air can go in the open end.

THINGS YOU WILL NEED:

- **2 adults**
- large garage or basement
- thin (0.5 mil), large trash bag
- electric hot plate
- gloves
- large rubber balloon
- small funnel
- hot tap water
- twist tie
- plastic pail
- cold water

2 When the bag is filled with hot air, a second adult can unplug the hot plate and help release the bag. What happens to the bag?

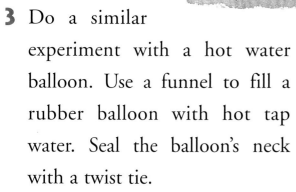

3 Do a similar experiment with a hot water balloon. Use a funnel to fill a rubber balloon with hot tap water. Seal the balloon's neck with a twist tie.

4 Put the balloon in a pail of cold water. What happens? Why did the hot air balloon float in colder air? Why did the hot water balloon float in cold water?

Balloons, Sky, and Water
An Explanation

A balloon full of hot air weighs less than a balloon full of cold air. A balloon full of hot water weighs less than a balloon full of cold water. As you saw, things that weigh less for the same space they take up float in things that weigh more.

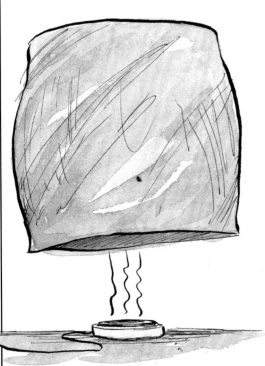

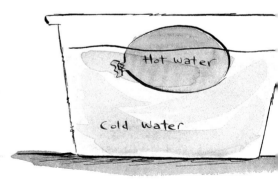

FACT: Balloonists burned bottled gas to heat the air that fills these beautiful balloons.

Ideas for Your Science Fair 🎀

- Use an eyedropper to add a drop of colored hot water to some cold water in a small glass. Predict what will happen. What will happen if you add a drop of colored cold water to hot water?

- Will a balloon filled with cold water float or sink in salt water? Does it matter how much salt is in the water?

Words to Know

air—An invisible mixture of gases that takes up space and has weight. One liter of air at sea level and 0° Celsius (32° Fahrenheit) weighs 1.29 grams.

air pressure—The weight of the air pushing on surfaces creates a pressure—a push that presses on all surfaces in air. Air pressure can be measured with a barometer.

clouds—A large number of tiny droplets of water. Clouds form when moisture (water) in the air cools and collects on tiny particles in the air.

constellation—A group of stars that forms a pattern in the sky. Astronomers have named 88 constellations.

scattering of light—When white light passes through small particles such as air or smoke, the particles soak up the cooler colors (violet, blue, green). Then they release this light in all directions. Much less of the warmer colors is soaked up. Scattering explains our blue sky and red sunsets.

stars—Objects in the sky, such as our sun, that give off light.

white light—Light from the sun is white. It is a mixture of all the colors you see in a rainbow.

Further Reading

Books

Bochinski, Julianne Blair. *The Complete Workbook for Science Fair Projects*. New York: John Wiley and Sons, 2005.

Dispezio, Michael A. *Super Sensational Science Fair Projects*. New York: Sterling Publishing, 2002.

Driscoll, Michael. *A Child's Introduction to the Night Sky*. New York: Black Dog & Leventhal Publishers, Inc., 2004.

Prinja, Raman. *Stars and Constellations*. Chicago: Heinemann Library, 2003.

Rhatigan, Joe, and Rain Newcomb. *Out-of-This-World Astronomy: 50 Amazing Activities & Projects*. New York: Lark Books, 2003.

Vogt, Gregory L. *Constellations*. Mankato, Minn.: Bridgestone Books, 2003.

Internet Addresses

Science News for Kids: Space and Astronomy.
<http://www.sciencenewsforkids.org/articles/20041201/refs.asp>

Science Projects for Kids.
<http://www.sciencemadesimple.com>

Index